Table of Contents

Written by Daniel Ho

Edited by Lydia Miyashiro-Ho

Photography by Lydia Miyashiro-Ho

Published by Daniel Ho Creations
914 Westwood Boulevard #813
Los Angeles, CA 90024
www.DanielHo.com

ISBN: 0-9842928-8-8 EAN: 978-0-9842928-8-2

Keanuhea

A lullaby for Kaleo. Ke aloha nō.

Rubato

by Daniel Ho

Haiku

The spirituality of this traditional Japanese poetic art form served as the inspiration for this composition. Use ponticello and vibrato to emulate the tone and musical inflections of a koto. The fast passages in measures 25-32 utilize hammer-ons and pull-offs to minimize plucking by the right hand.

♩ = 75

by Daniel Ho

15
f
18
mp
poco a poco cresc. to measure 25
22
f
25
ff
27
29
fff

ritard
a tempo
poco a poco decresc. to end
ritard
fine

Kauanoenoe

The light misty rain is a metaphor of hope. It refracts sunlight into rainbow-colored sparkles, inviting us to see everything around us anew. It nourishes new growth with its tears of happiness. There is no grief in the light misty rain, only anticipation and fortitude to carry on as if every day were a new beginning.

Rubato

by Daniel Ho

rubato
a tempo

40
44
48
52
rubato
56
a tempo
mf
mp

rubato
ritard
p
fine

♩ = 95

Bicycle Holiday

Freewheeling with the wind in your face.

by Daniel Ho

mp
mf

rubato
fine

On a Gentle Island Breeze

Like the breeze, this melody moves in waves. It stops and starts like phrases of the wind with inner melodies weaving throughout.

Daniel Ho

f
mp
mf
fine

Amis Rondo

This whirlwind-like rondo was written in the key of "Ami"
to recognize the indigenous Amis tribe of Taiwan.

Daniel Ho

Allegro

ritard
ritard
rubato

a tempo
mf
dim. & ritard
poco a poco cresc. & accel.
presto
mf

77
81
85
f
89
93
97
mf
101

106
111
115
119
124
128
133

dim. & ritard
rubato
ritard
ritard
fine

Pua Kea Waltz *(White Flower Waltz)*

The delicate dance of the twirling tung flower is set to the lilt of an ʻukulele waltz.

by Daniel Ho

rubato

D.S. al Coda
dim.
ritard
fine

Jesu, Joy of Man's Desiring

Originally scored for voices, trumpet, oboes, strings, and continuo, this 'ukulele duet is an excellent exercise for hammer-ons and pull-offs.

Johann Sebastian Bach
arrangement by Daniel Ho

22
1
2
27
31

35
39
43
1
2

47
1
2
51
55

59
63
67
ritard
fine

Two Part Invention No. 8

BWV 779

Listen to how the two 'ukuleles interact—sometimes they answer each other;
at other times they play together in harmony.

Johann Sebastian Bach
arrangement by Daniel Ho

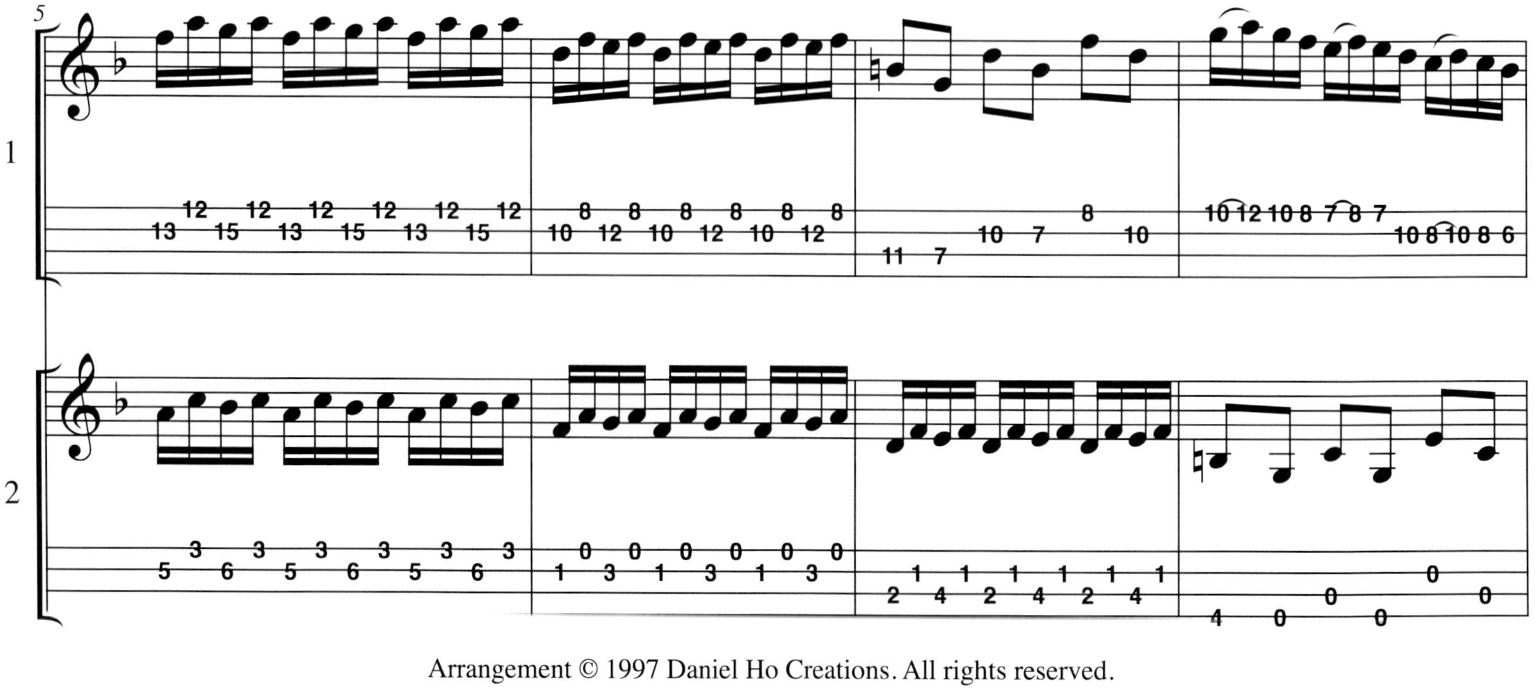

9
1
2
14
1
2
18
1
2

ritard
fine
ritard
fine

Two Part Invention No. 13

BWV 784

On the album ***'Ukulele Classics & Originals****, the lower parts of these Bach duets are panned to the left speaker and the higher parts to the right speaker in an effort to clearly distinguish them from one another. The ability to hear the intricacies of Bach's melodies promotes a deeper appreciation of his contrapuntal writing.*

Johann Sebastian Bach
arrangement by Daniel Ho

Uke 1

Uke 2

1

2

8
1
2
11
1
2
14
1
2

17
1
2
20
1
2
23
1
ritard
fine
2
ritard
fine

School's Out

Elements of Latin music capture the relief and excitement a child might feel when the buzzer rings... School's Out!

♩= 108

by Daniel Ho

10
E E/G♯ A B E E/G♯ F♯mi B/D♯
1
2
mf
14
E E/G♯ A B C♯mi E/G♯ F♯mi E B/D♯ B C♯mi E
1
2
3
18
A/E E E6 E A E/G♯
1
strum
2

F♯mi
E
A
E/G♯
F♯mi
E
A/E E
E6 E
A/E E
fingerstyle
strum
B/E
E
A/E E
E6 E
A/E E

34
B/E
E
A
E/G♯
F♯mi
1
2
fingerstyle
38
E
A
E/G♯
F♯mi
42
E
A
E/G♯
F♯mi

46
E
A
E
E/G♯
1
2
mp
mf
52
A
B
E
E/G♯
F♯mi
B
E
E/G♯
A
B
strum
f
57
C♯mi
E/G♯
F♯mi
B/D♯
B
E
E/G♯
A
B
fingerstyle
mf

61
E E/G♯ F♯mi B E E/G♯ A B
65
C♯mi E/G♯ F♯mi E B/D♯ B C♯mi E
A/E E
69
A E/G♯ F♯mi E

73
A
E/G♯
F♯mi
E
1
2
77
solo
A
E/G♯
F♯mi
E
A
strum
82
E/G♯
F♯mi
no chord
fingerstyle

87
1
2
91
strum
E
E/G♯
A
B
F♯mi
solo
96
C♯mi
G♯mi
F♯mi E
B/D♯
B
C♯mi
fingerstyle
fine

Pineapple Mango

(solo 'ukulele)

I wrote ***Pineapple Mango*** *while enrolled in the Composing and Arranging Program at the Grove School of Music. We were taught to write in many commercial styles, and this was my assignment for "TV Main Title" week. In 2007, Amy Ku'uleialoha Stillman wrote lyrics to this melody and it took on a new life as* ***The Breakfast Song****. Nowadays, I enjoy watching the various cover performances of this piece on YouTube.*

by Daniel Ho

D G G C D G
G C D G G verse C
D G G C
D G G C D G
G C D G
chorus G C D G G C

D
G
G
C
D
G
G
C
D
G
solo
G
C
D
G
G
C
D
G
G
C
D
G
G
C
D
G
fine

The Breakfast Song *(Pineapple Mango)*

On preparing breakfast when you're not yet fully awake.

♩= 164

by Amy Ku'uleialoha Stillman & Daniel Ho

Pineapple Mango *('ukulele accompaniment)*

The following parts are accompaniments for the solo 'ukulele arrangement of *Pineapple Mango,* or its version with lyrics, *The Breakfast Song*.

The song is based on a four bar chord progression (G, C, D, G), so any part can be played in any section of the song.

In an ensemble, the parts can be layered together in various combinations to create unique arrangements.

♩= 164

Verse - This is the intro of the solo 'ukulele arrangment. Originally a bass line, it ascends to a higher register to create an eight bar phrase. It works well in the verses.

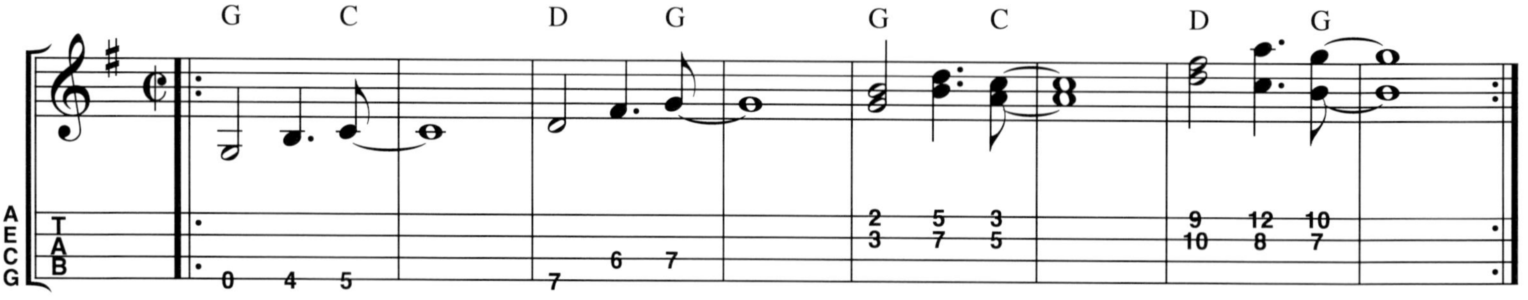

Chorus - Emulate an upright bass by muting the strings with your right palm. This busier pattern adds energy to the chorus sections.

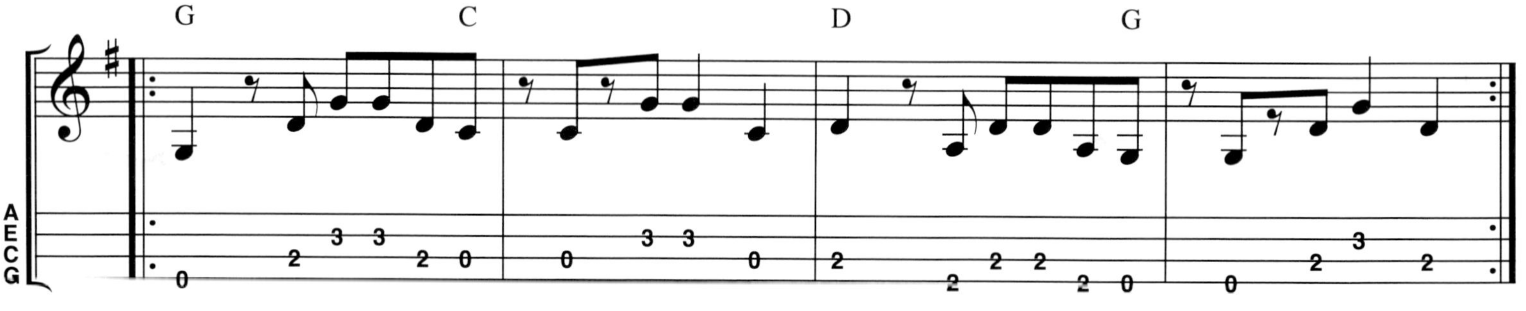

Strum - Notice the melody weaving through the chords. Use a muted strum where the accents are marked. Keep your right hand moving down and up in a consistent eighth note rhythm throughout.

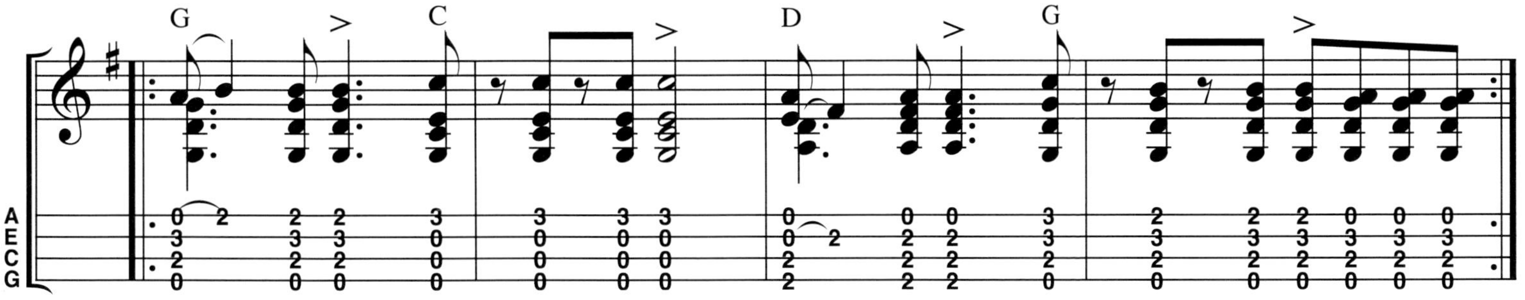

Fingerstyle - Imagine a Latin piano feel when playing the following part.

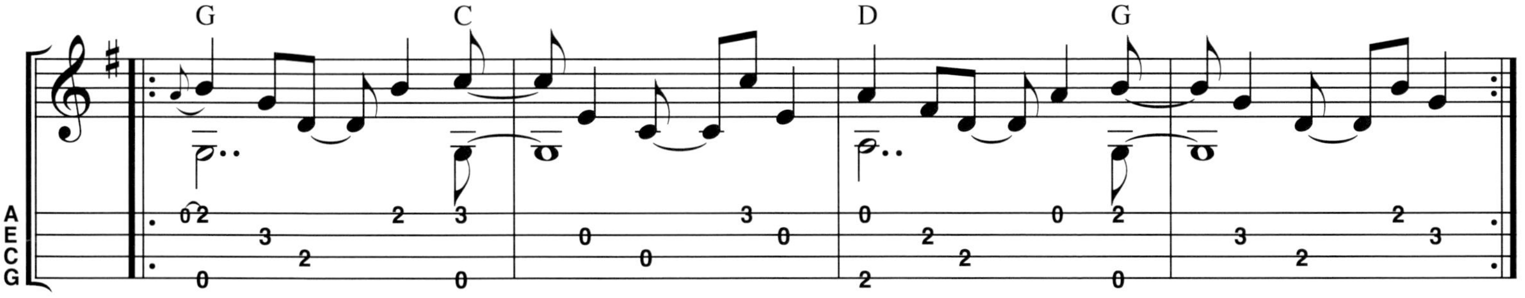

Harmonics - Finger the notes with your left hand while quickly touching the same string twelve frets higher with your right index finger and plucking it with your right thumb.

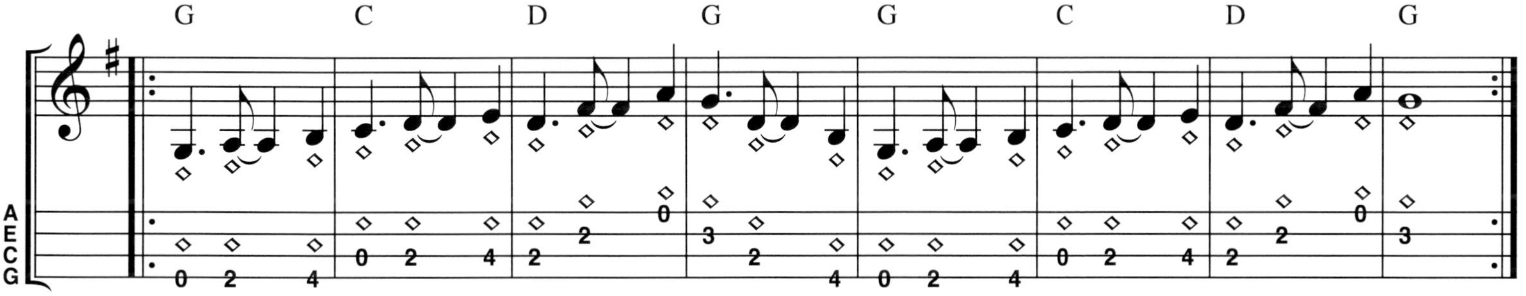

Percussion - The Mozambique rhythm originated in Cuba. The right hand plays a cowbell or agogo bell pattern while the left hand plays a bass line using hammer-ons.

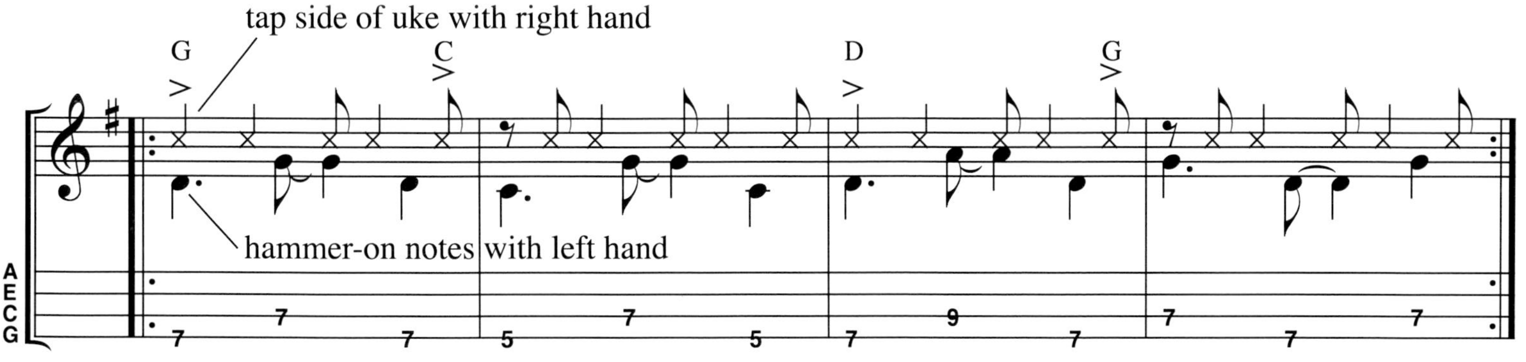

For Eternity

♩ = 117

uke strum simile throughout...

by Hope Mayo & Daniel Ho

51 E♭ma7 Gmi7 C
warm For e - ter - ni - ty For e - ter - ni - ty
safe and warm
55 F Ami Gmi7 C
bop mm-bah-dop mm - bah-dop bah bah-mm-bah dah-bop bop bah
59 F Ami Gmi7 C
bop mm-bah-dop mm - bah-dop bah bah-mm-bah dah-bop bop bah
63 F Ami Gmi7 3 C
An-oth - er day as this dream fades a - way
67 Gmi7 3 C Ami D7
as the tides wash a - way all I be-lieved in you and you in me
71 Gmi7 C F F7 B♭ C
for e-ter - ni-ty And when the sand had turned to stone
77 F Dmi B♭ C
we did-n't know which way to go It seems as though our love was washed a way
81 F F7 B♭ C F
Our sun has set the nights are cold I'm here with you and all
86 Dmi E♭ma7 Gmi7 C
a - lone to - night For e - ter - ni - ty for e - ter - ni - ty
91 F Ami Gmi7 C
bop mm-bah-dop mm - bah-dop bah bah-mm-bah dah-bop bop bah
95 F Ami Gmi7 C F
bop mm-bah-dop mm - bah-dop bah bah-mm-bah dah-bop bop bah
fine

♩= 146

Living In Paradise

by Faith Rivera & Daniel Ho

A
vocal
E
Eat - ing out one day I heard some - bod - y say, "gee
Down-town to Ka - po - lei on the H - 1 Free - way I'm
D
A
things ain't like what they used to be"
stuck (a - lone) in a sea of lone - ly driv - ers
A
E
I work three times as hard car's rust - ing in the yard and my
There's so much fish in the sea why then is there on - ly me? I

25
D
A
house (our house) ain't worth half what it used to be
wish (some - one) would share this ride with me
29
D
A
Things are chang-ing all a - round the mar - ket's up the mar - ket's down
Then I'd be in the car - pool lane cruis - ing by with the rad - i - o playing
33
B mi
E sus
but hey we're liv - ing in pa-ra - dise and it's cool cool cool yeah
the sun is out and I'm just a - long for the ri - i - ide yeah

A E F♯mi D
Oo - oo oo - oo oo - oo I got the sun in my eyes
A E F♯mi D
Oo - oo oo - oo oo - oo dream-in' on a clear blue
A E F♯mi D
sky Oo - oo oo - oo oo - oo got the sun in my

49
A
E
D
eyes Oo - oo oo - oo
liv-ing in pa-ra-dise
53
A
E
F♯mi
D
uke solo
57
A
E
F♯mi
D

61
A
E
F♯mi
D
65
A
E
D
69
A
E
F♯mi
D
Oo - oo oo - oo oo - oo got the sun in my
strum

73
A E F♯mi D
eyes Oo - oo oo - oo oo - oo
gon-na be dream-ing of a
77
A E F♯mi D
Oo - oo oo - oo oo - oo such a clear
clear blue sky
81
A E
1.
D
Oo - oo oo - oo
blue sky

85
2.
D
A
D/A
liv-ing here in pa-ra-dise
89
E/A
D/A
A
mp
92
D/A
E/A
D/A
A
fine
ritard

Along for the Ride

♩ = 102

by Faith Rivera & Daniel Ho

Csus4 C Bb C
I'm just a-long for the ride
And there's no need for me
f
Dm Bb F Bb
to drive oh no I'm just a-long for the ride
I'm hap-py tak-ing in all
Dm F/C C Bb C
the sights oh I'm just a-long for the just a-long for the ride
mf
F Bb C F Bb C
do do do do do
You in-sist I should
F Bb C F
have some di-rec-tion Take a stand take con-trol
Bb C F Gm Bb
Here's my two cents Mis-ter Bus-man drive me a-way oh

42
C sus4 C B♭ C F
an-y-where please 'Cause I'm on the bus go-ing no - where fast
45
B♭ C F B♭ C
I missed my stop but it's O - K My prized pos-ses-sion is my
48
D m B♭ C sus4 C
Mick-ey Mouse watch oh I like it this way I tell ya I'm just a-long for the ride
D.S. al Coda
52
F uke solo B♭ C F
55
B♭ C F B♭ C

58
F 3 Bb C Bb C
You might not ap-prove of this
mf
61
F Bb C F
road I'm travel-ing My life is like a Sun - day drive
64
Bb C Dm Bb
But thanks for ask-ing 'bout me an - y - way I'll be al - right I like it this way
67
C sus4 C Bb
I'm just a - long for the ride
f
70
C Dm Bb
And there's no need for me to drive oh no I'm just a - long for the ride
73
F Bb Dm F/C
I'm hap-py tak-ing in all the sights oh I'm just a-long for the

77
C
F/C
C
just a-long for the ride
just a-long for the
just a-long for the ride
80
D♭
E♭
F
just a-long for the
just a-long for the ride
ff
83
B♭
C
F
B♭
C
I'm on the bus go-ing no-where a-long for the
86
F
B♭
C
F
ride
Don't like the road that I'm
89
B♭
C
F
1.
B♭
C
travel-ing but I'll be al-right
92
2.
B♭
C
rubato
F
A-long for the ride
fine

Cup of Joe

♩= 90

by Lydia Miyashiro-Ho & Daniel Ho

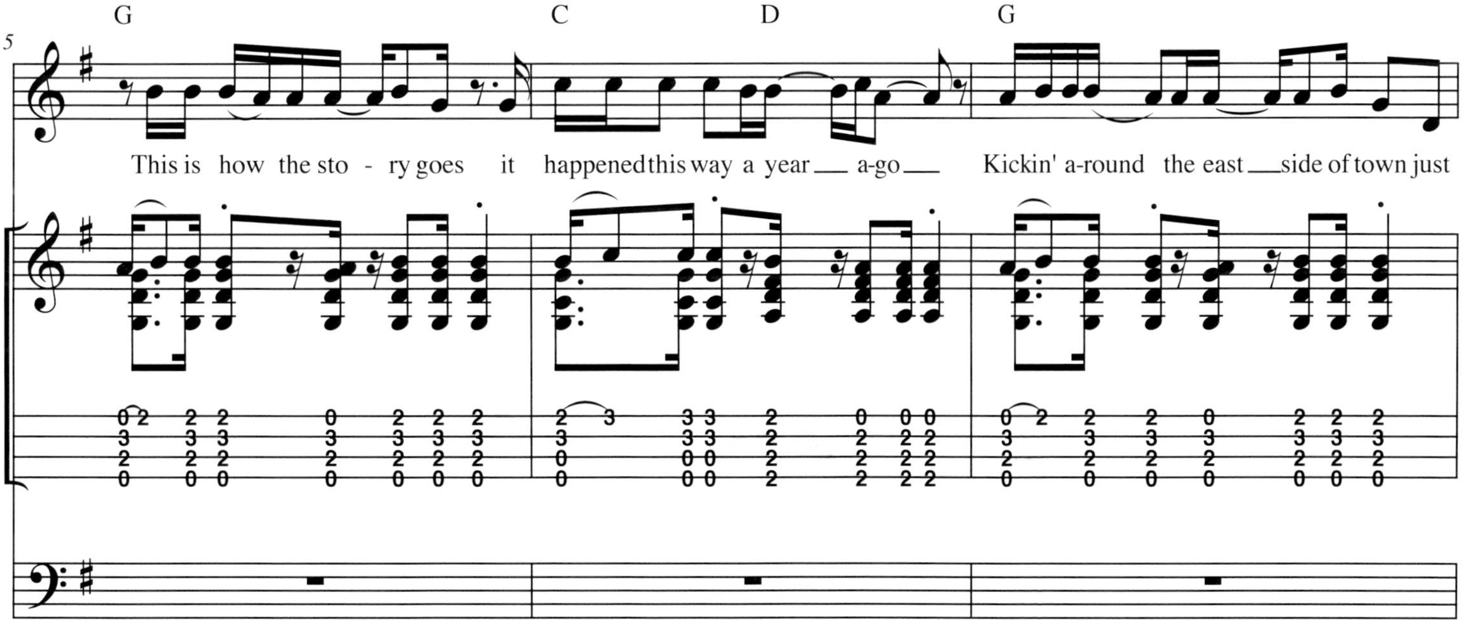

C D G C D 3
8
me so - lo Enter stage right cap-puc-ci-no in hand the prin-cess of my fair-y-tale
G C D G
11
Had to find a way to be her man some way some - how I wan-na be your cup of joe the
mp
C D G C D
14
first sip in the morn - in' Your get you goin' ri-tu-al and warm your soul from with-in

17
G
C
D
G
Let me be your cup of joe the first sip in the morn - in' Ba-by take me as I am and through your
20
C
D
G
C
D
veins I'll be flow - - - - in'
muted picking
23
G
C
D
G
Her hair so long the tow - er so high
strum
mf

26
C D G C D
a lone-ly tree a-gainst ___ a black sky Shards of my shat-tered heart ___ still shine with ___ hope ___
29
G C D
Pup-py dog close: you can try me on and if you're not hap-py then I'll ___ be gone Have a
31
G C D
drink of your dou-ble ca-fe mo-cha with soy It's get - ting ___ cold ___
8va

33
G C D G
I wanna be your cup of joe the first sip in the morn - in' Your get you goin' ri-tu-al and warm your
36
C D G C D
soul from with-in Let me be your cup of joe the first sip in the morn - in' Ba-by
39
G C D G
take me as I am and through your veins I'll be flow - - - - in'
uke solo
f

C D G
C D G C D
G C D G
Fun-ny how the sto - ry ends we
strum
mp

50
C D G C D
tried to get a-long as friends Guess it was-n't meant to be no way no how
mp
53
G C D G
Done in from the mo - ment we met ev-er af - ter you and me on Luck-y stars we made our bet so
56
C D G C D
hap - pi - ly I wan-na be your cup of joe the first sip in the morn - in' Your
mf

G C D G
get you goin' ri-tu-al and warm your soul from with-in
Let me be your cup of joe the
C D G C D
first sip in the morn - in' Ba-by take me as I am and through your veins I'll be flow - - -
G C D G
lead vocal ad lib
I wan-na be your cup of joe the first sip in the morn - in'

C D G C D
Let me be your cup of joe the first sip in the morn - in'
G C D G
lead vocal ad lib
muted picking
C D G C D G
fine

Aloha Pumehana

by Amy Ku'uleialoha Stillman & Daniel Ho

Pua I Ka Ua

(Flowers in the Rain)

♩ = 184

by Amy Ku'uleialoha Stillman & Daniel Ho

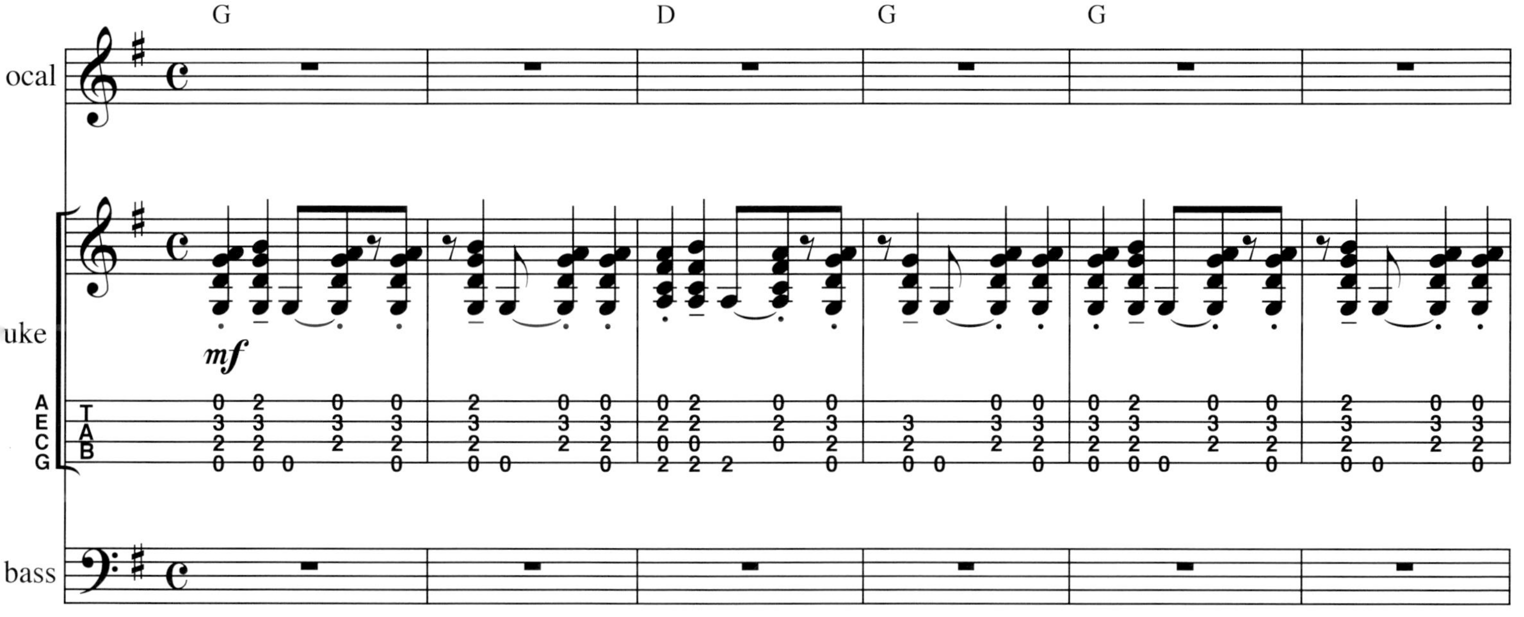

13
G D G G
pu - a he pu - a he pu-a na - ni e
strum
mf
19
D G G D G
He
25
G D G G
pu - a he pu - a he pu-a i mo - ha - la He pu - a he pu - a he

31
D G G D G
pu - a na - ni e
harmonics
37
G D G G
'E - lu - a 'e - lu - a 'e -
harmonics
43
D G G D G
lu - a ma - u pu - a 'E - lu - a 'e - lu - a 'e - lu - a pu - a e

49
G D G G
55
D G G D G
Ka - u - a ka - u - a e 'o - hi i na pu - a Ka -
strum
61
G D G A
u - a ka - u - a e 'o - hi ma - i e
tap side of uke
hammer-on

67
E A A E A
He
73
A E A A
u-a he u-a e i-ho mai ka u-a He u-a he u-a e
79
E A A E A
i-ho ma-i e

85
A E A A
Pu - a - na pu - a - na ke -
91
E A A E A
i - a mo - 'o - le - lo 'E - lu - a ka - u - a mau pu - a na - ni e
97
A E A A
strum

103
E A A E A
Pu - a - na pu - a - na ke - i - a mo - 'o - le - lo 'E -
109
A E A A
lu - a ka - u - a mau pu - a na - ni e
tap side of uke
hammer-on
115
E A A E A
fine
harmonics

Cookie Hula

♩ = 184

by Amy Ku'uleialoha Stillman & Daniel Ho

5
G C D C D G
9
G C D G
'O - ni a - na i ka choc - o - late 'a - mi a - na i ka
Ka - lu - a i ka oat - meal pi - pi - 'i i ka rai -
Po - ke - po - ke i ka pea - nut ka - wi - li i ka but -
Pa - 'i - pa - la - o - a ma - ka 'a - i a mo - mo -
Ha - 'i - na ka pu - a - na 'a - mi 'o - ni cook - ie

12
C D G C D
chip 'O - ni a - na i ka choc - o - late
- - sin Ka - lu - a i ka oat - meal
- - ter Po - ke - po - ke i ka pea - nut
- - na Pa - 'i - pa - la - o - a ma - ka
hula Ha - 'i - na ka pu - a - na
15
C D G
repeat 4x
C D G
'a - mi a - na i ka chip
pi - pi - 'i i ka rai - sin
ka - wi - li i ka but - ter
'a - i a mo - mo - na
'a - mi 'o - ni cook - ie hula
'a - mi 'o - ni cook - ie hula
fine